D0546587

The Lighting
of the
Acolyte

A TREASURY OF BLUNDERS AND BLOOPERS
FROM CHURCH BULLETINS AND NEWSLETTERS

Linda M. Jump

CARTOONS BY
MARCIA KOZUBEK

C.S.S. Publishing Co., Inc.

Lima, Ohio

LIGHTING OF THE ACOLYTE

*To David and the congregation at Elm Park,
who are able to conduct worship each Sunday despite my foibles*

and

*To Dick, Jennifer and Allison, who cherish
me in spite of all my bloopers*

Copyright © 1987 by
The C.S.S. Publishing Company, Inc.
Lima, Ohio

All rights reserved. No part of this publication may be reproduced, stored in a retrieval system, or transmitted in any form or by any means, electronic, mechanical, photocopying, recording, or otherwise, without the prior permission of the publisher. Inquiries should be addressed to: The C.S.S. Publishing Company, Inc., 628 South Main Street, Lima, Ohio 45804.

Library of Congress Cataloging-in-Publication Data

Jump, Linda M., 1950-
    The lighting of the acolyte.

    1. Religion — Anecdotes, facetiae, satire, etc.
    2. Errors and blunders, Literary.   I. Title.
PN6231.R4J8   1987   818'.5402   87-15085
ISBN 0-89536-896-X

Contents

Preface

This book represents a labor of love. The idea for the book germinated the day I made the first blooper of this book. A Presbyterian church secretary (who comes weekly to use our stencil cutter) shared a laugh and then topped mine with her own sermon title blooper that also appears in the book.

Within minutes, a fellow United Methodist secretary called and I asked if she had any funny typos to share with us. Those three were the impetus for the book, as I realized every secretary (and pastor) has a humorous story to share.

I wrote to thousands of church secretaries across the United States, serving six major denominations and I placed advertisements in church publications. The bloopers quickly rolled in. My pastor, friends and I couldn't wait for the next day's mail to see if other secretaries were as human as I. Thanks to each church secretary and pastor who took time from overwhelming schedules to share stories or typos. I'm just sorry I couldn't use all received, but dozens were similar, a few were "X" rated and some just plain were not as funny as others.

Church secretaries could blame the typewriter, word processor, proof reader or pastor's handwriting, but the truth is, the connection between the brain and paper causes these bloopers. These are unintentional typos that are only funny after the shock that we are human enough to have made such a secular error wears off.

But, if the Lord loveth a cheerful giver, church bloopers just might be part of a plan to keep church members amused before the offering! At least, I pray they serve some noble cause, since there seems to be a variety in our churches. Enjoy these!

Lighting of the Acolyte

"Lighting of the acolyte"

(See page 7)

1

Typing the church bulletin among telephone calls, visitors and the requests of the pastor can make for some amusing, but embarrassing errors. One Sunday, I typed "Lighting of", intending to complete that phrase with "The Candles" and the name of the acolyte for the week. Unfortunately, two calls interrupted my task and when I returned to type, I copied a previous bulletin which used the term "acolyte." I typed that in, as well as the child's name. I was horrified, but also tickled by what I had typed:

Lighting of the Acolyte   Kimberly Lockwood

"Lighting of the acolyte"

This appeared in a May church bulletin:

"This summer, you can visit another country in your own living room! Become a host family for a foreign student for three weeks through INTERSTUD. For more information, contact Miss Macaire Henderson at (phone number listed)."

While the message appears to promote international

8

hanky-panky, it should have encouraged a study exchange program.

Shared by Pam McKinley, secretary
Lutheran Church of the Good Shepherd
Holmdel, NJ

A Pennsylvania church secretary was typing a bulletin message asking that mothers desiring to have children baptized contact the pastor. When a single word was dropped, the message became:

"Those mothers desiring to have children, please contact the pastor."

Shared by a previous pastor
Mansfield United Methodist Church
Mansfield, PA

Our church building is large, and when I became secretary, it took my predecessor nearly an hour to explain the key system. On the back of a door in the church office, each key was neatly labeled with a letter and number to match a large floor plan of the church. All the exits and closet doors were labeled to correspond to one of the keys. The system seemed foolproof for quickly finding the right key to each church lock. But at the bottom of the neat rows of keys were a half dozen odd-shaped keys that weren't individually labeled.

"What are these for?" I asked. The former secretary shrugged and said they were extras that didn't seem to fit any of the doors. It was then I noticed she had appropriately labeled the group of keys: "Twilight Zone."

The bulletin of a Baptist church in Birmingham, Alabama carried this blooper:

"The deacons will all sin together in the first pew this morning."

Shared by a Birmingham secretary
Who requested anonymity

And all this time, we thought the number was unlisted except through prayer — Rather than type "Call Chris" with the proper telephone number, a Poughkeepsie, New York secretary instead typed:
"Call Christ (with the phone number)"

Shared by Judy Williams, secretary
Community United Methodist Church
Poughkeepsie, NY

This message with a double-meaning appeared in a parish publication:
"Ginny Howard is our new flower chairperson. She will be taking dates after the service in the social hall."

Shared by Ros Parrish, secretary
United Church of Pittsford
Pittsford, NY

The small United Methodist Church did not have indoor plumbing, though it did have a well. Because of the inconvenience of going outside into the harsh Pennsylvania winter air, the pastor suggested a fund drive for an indoor bathroom. The committee was less than enthusiastic. "The water would freeze," one member said, remembering that the church was only heated on Sundays. So, the pastor suggested a chemical toilet like those on airplanes.
"Not on the airline I was on," one member drawled, "There was a sign that said, 'do not flush until over a wooded area.' "
An older member, who lived his entire life in the

mountains, took offense. He barked, "Huh, doesn't pay to be a hunter these days!"

Shared by Rev. Douglas N. Akers,
Oneonta District Superintendent
United Methodist Church
Sidney, NY

New Year's Eve happened to fall on a Sunday, so the secretary of a Kansas church decided to use an extra line at the bottom of the last page of the bulletin to type "Have a Happy New Year!"

It was the end of a hectic day, and she mistyped: "Have a Hairy New Year!"

Shared by Doris R. Koepsel, secretary
Trinity Lutheran Church
Abilene, KS

It was during a busy Christmas season that one of the members of the church, who was a favorite of the church secretary was hospitalized. Instead of typing that "Mary Christman" was hospitalized, the secretary typed the name as "Mary Christmas."

Shared by Eleanor M. Berger, secretary
St. John's Evangelical Lutheran Church
Kutztown, PA

A pastor served an extremely small country church, whose building was heated by coal heaters and whose plumbing was outside. The tiny congregation usually consisted of fewer than a dozen women at least sixty-five years old.

The church sat on a beautiful mountainside overlooking a picturesque valley. An old, abandoned dirt road ran from the church beside the mountain into the thick forest. Often, the pastor drove to church early, leaving the car in the parking lot to walk down the dirt road into the forest to commune with deer, wild turkeys and God.

One morning, however, the pastor was lost in the serenity of the place and realized he would be late starting the service. As he approached the church, the usual congregation of elderly women hovered near the outhouse. The pastor expected to be chastized for his tardiness, but instead, was greeted with sighs of relief. The women had seen the pastor's car and, not finding him in the church, thought something had happened to him while he was in the outhouse. The elderly women had been arguing for several minutes over who would have to check on him in the outhouse. They were so glad to see him, they forgot how late he was!

Shared by Rev. Rees F. Warring, senior pastor
Elm Park United Methodist Church
Scranton, PA

Pastor, are you in there?

Zion Church advertised a pig roast and visit to a nearby petting zoo in a bulletin announcement that raised a few eyebrows. It read:

"Purchase of ticket provides: pig, buns, dessert, beverage and entertainment (hayride, petting, too!)"

Shared by Clarence Larson, member
Zion Lutheran Church
Belvidere, IL (now living in Mission, TX)

The caption across the bottom of the church bulletin of a young, rapidly growing congregation was puzzling. The pastor intended to remind parishioners that there was no money for hiring help, so new and regular attendees were enlisted to take positions of active responsibility. But, instead of reading, "There's a job in this church for you," the message read:
"There's a jo*n* in this church for you."

Shared by Ron Fuller, secretary
Eastwood Baptist Church
Medford, OR

The young people of the First Baptist Church had gatherings after the evening service to serve soft drinks, sing and visit. One Sunday, they also swam. Intending to say "sip," the bulletin read, "Sin n' Sing n' Swim."

Shared by LeeDel Howard, secretary
First Baptist Church
Wichita, KS

Is this an indication of their giving? During the ritual of friendship, members of a New York church were asked to sign a sheet in the pew. Instead, the secretary asked members to:
"Please *sigh* during offering."

Shared by Barbara A. Merritt, secretary
First United Methodist Church
Minoa, NY

The list of youth helpers at a Connecticut church included *Demon* Butterworth. The name should have been Damon, but sometimes typos are actually appropriate.

Shared by Yvonne Dee Wallace, secretary
First United Methodist Church
Middletown, CT

The spirit is abundant in this church! The bulletin of a New York church carried this message:

"The flowers on the altar are given by Norm and Audrey Johnson in memory of his parents and her father. They are our greeters."

Who are the greeters, asked parishioners — the deceased relatives?

Shared by Ros Parrish, secretary
United Church of Pittsford
Pittsford, NY

The church bulletin was announcing a congregational rummage sale. It invited members to "a preview of our *bizarre*."

Shared by Lonny Gulden, member
Peace Lutheran Church
Bloomington, MN

It was the Lakewood United Methodist Church's turn to provide food for the needy, but the bulletin supplement instead listed the weekly needs under the following headline:

"Millcreek Food Panty"

Shared by Delores Hooven, secretary
Lakewood United Methodist Church
Erie, PA

After a hectic Easter season with a doubled work load and plenty of extra bulletins to produce, the church secretary at Trinity Lutheran Church typed:

"Church office will be closed Monday. Halleluia. Halleluia."

Shared by Daisy Nethero, secretary
Trinity Lutheran Church
Jackson, MS

Do you have to be bi-sexual to attend? For two years, Elm Park Church offered a weekly mild exercise class for women over age 55. The program was sponsored by the Office for the Aging, which is housed in the church. In typing a notice saying that for the first time, an exercise class for men over 55 would be offered as well, here is what I typed:

"The Senior Center now provides mild exercise classes for persons over age 55 who are both male and female."

An anniversary notice in a New York church took an interesting twist when the church secretary typed what sounded OK. She wrote:

"The flowers are given in honor of two special occasions: The 59th wedding anniversary of Edith and Bob Betchley; and, on the occasion of Howard Kuntz's retirement from his wife, Sue."

The pastor commented, "Is it cheaper than divorce?"

Shared by Kathy Bush, secretary
Farmingdale United Methodist Church
Farmingdale, NY

A Jewish leader was scheduled to lead in the worship service of a New York church. By adding a single letter, the secretary typed:

"It is with renewed delight that we welcome Rabbi*t* Hermann of Temple Emanu-El."

Shared by Linda Doughty, secretary
United Methodist Church of East Meadow
East Meadow, NY

Speaking of rabbis . . . One secretary reverted her Lutheran church to Old Testament practices with the slip of a letter:

"The sanctuary lamb (should have been lamp) burns

this week to the glory of God.''

Shared by Carol Barrett, secretary
Prince of Peace Lutheran Church
Marlton, NJ

"Come join us and sin in the choir."

The previous secretary of a California church made a common, but humorous error:
"Come join us and sin in the choir."

Shared by Betty Cheeseborough, secretary
First Christian Church
Visalia, CA

It's cold in South Dakota, but a prayer freeze? The Lake Campbell Lutheran Church of Volyn, a wee country church, carried this bulletin message in November:
"No more Bible study and prayer until spring because of the cold weather and driving conditions."

Shared by H. Conrad Hoyer, whose sister
attends
Lake Campbell Lutheran Church
Volyn, SD

A volunteer at a Michigan church normally word processes the bulletin on a home computer. While he was vacationing, the pastor decided to type it himself. But he found his sermon title — "A Tormented, Joyful Man" described his experience. He had the "Brief order for confession and *frog*iveness." The hymn of praise appeared as "This is the *b*east" and a second hymn "Lamb of *dog*."

Shared by Rev. Ronald E. McCallum, pastor
St. Luke's Lutheran Church
Stevensville, MI

A Michigan church bulletin carried this double-meaning message:
"Today has been designated as World Hunger Sunday because of the church picnic next week."

Shared by John G. Lundborg
St. Luke's Lutheran Church
Muskegon, MI

A Presbyterian church in Ohio, housed next door to a youth rehabilitation center, made a blooper that received a number of comments. Rather than list the ushers one Sunday, the secretary listed the names as being "users."

Shared by Norma K. Ahlborn, secretary
Central College Church
Central College, OH

The "Who's Serving This Week" page of the bulletin of a North Carolina church carried a list of the ushers. When one letter was omitted from the title of the assistant usher, the name was listed as the "ass."

Shared by Debra J. Stallings, secretary
St. James Lutheran Church
Concord, NC

A Maryland Baptist church is the place for

17

cannibalistic members. Ushers there *eat* people, not seat them.

Shared by Elsie Fleming, secretary
Mount Calvary Baptist Church
Rock Valley, MD

Better arrive on time at this Maryland church. Joining many churches, the First Baptist Church uses asterisks next to some lines in the church bulletin to designate places where ushers will seat latecomers. But a typo changed the wording. At the end of the bulletin, it read: "Ushers will *swat* the latecomers."

Shared by Harold R. Price, former minister
of music
First Baptist Church
Rockville, MD now of Harrisburg, PA

In a similar error, a Pennsylvania church, rather than list seating intervals to indicate when latecomers would be seated by ushers listed "searing intervals." One member was concerned she had missed something by arriving on time.

Shared by Gloria Schrock, secretary
St. Paul's United Methodist Church
Warrington, PA

A clergy couple in Idaho took turns preaching. When the husband was slated for an out-of-town meeting, the bulletin read:

"Next week, Barbara will be preaching on temptation while David is away."

Shared by Rev. Barbara Bellus Upp
then co-pastor, Filer United Meth. Church
Filer, ID
now at Asbury United Methodist Church
Hood River, OR

They don't give striped uniforms? Without realizing what she had typed, a California secretary inserted this message:

"I was naked and in jail and you visited me."

Shared by Louise Fredriksz, secretary
Alum Rock United Methodist Church
San Jose, CA

Need Four-Year-Old

"German shepherd"

(See page 23)

2

Ruth, four years old, returned from church school to inform her parents that Chuck Davey, the church school superintendent, is Jesus. Startled at that revelation, her mother asked why. "Well," Ruth answered, "we sing the song 'hear our pennies dropping, count them one by one, every one for Jesus' and then Mr. Davey comes around and collects them. He must be Jesus."

Shared by Ruth's brother, Rev. Douglas Akers
Oneonta District Superintendent
United Methodist Church
Sidney, NY

"This doesn't spell STAR."

A Baptist church school class was presenting a nativity play and four children were designated to hold letters to a song about the Star of Bethlehem. Unfortunately, the first child, carrying the letter "S," went stage left instead of right. The children sang beautifully, as the parents roared. The children's letters spelled: R-A-T-S.

Shared by James F. Tompkins, member
First Baptist Church
Oneonta, NY

Typing what some women may think about providing child care during the worship service, a New York church posted the following in the Easter bulletin:

"Nursery is available at *bother* services this morning."

Shared by Lana Roske, secretary
Vestal United Methodist Church
Vestal, NY

A letter to the parents of church-school children of a New Jersey church carried this message:

"The year has gone well to this point; but since Easter, there has been a significant drop off in attendance. It is at this point we need your *newed assistance.*"

The secretary did not mean naked attendance as requested, but *RE-newed* assistance.

Shared by Barbara Delman, secretary
Holy Cross Lutheran Church
Toms River, NJ

I guess if you start them teaching at a young age, you have a good supply — The Luther Memorial Church in Syracuse, New York posted the following announcement:

"Due to personal schedule changes, we find ourselves in need of a four-year-old assistant Sunday School teacher . . ."

Shared by Bruce L. Reagan, member
Luther Memorial Church
N. Syracuse, NY

My daughter Allison joined the church school classes in singing a song called *Good News* during the worship service. She was singing in the car to learn the words and to share the song with us. I was puzzled by one line: "Oppossums, disciples and fair donkeys. His family, his friends, and his enemies."

It was Sunday morning before I realized the line was "Apostles, disciples, and Pharisees."

Jake, a kindergartener, was learning the Bible story of the shepherd who left his 99 sheep in search of a single lost lamb. Jake told his mother he learned about a shepherd in church school. "What kind of shepherd was he?" the mother asked, prompting the child to tell her about the sheep. Jake scuffed his shoe on the floor and looked down in thought.

Then his face brightened. "It must have been a German Shepherd," he exclaimed.

Shared by Linda S. Biggs, member
Elm Park United Methodist Church
Oneonta, NY

"German shepherd"

I was teaching the first and second grade church school class about the nativity and showed them a traditional picture of Mary holding Jesus in the stable scene. "Where's Joseph?" one boy asked. A second child quickly responded, "Who do you think took the picture, silly?"

A registration form for the night Vacation Bible

School intended to seek a person to call in case of emergency. A typo changed one line to:
"In case of *emergence*, who should be contacted?"
The mother, of course, said the pastor.

Shared by Sandra Viands, secretary
Charles Town Presbyterian Church
Charles Town, WV

The adult education announcement in an Oregon church was really not done for effect, the secretary insists. The class about the denomination was entitled, "How Do You Spell Presbyterian?" The secretary blooped and typed this:
"How Do You Spell Presbyterina?"

Shared by Mary Burke, secretary
First Presbyterian Church
Medford, OR

A list of instructions sent to teachers by the nursery school secretary in a church said:
"Please ask early arrivals to *wail* on the chairs in the hallway at Zion or the big room at Liebenzell."

Shared by Linda Matson, secretary
Zion Lutheran Church
Long Valley, NJ

Pastor John
Meets
the Broads

"*Getting rid of the guilts.*"

(See page 29)

3

Not just church bulletins, but church newsletters are full of humorous typographical errors. A favorite comes from a Colorado Disciples of Christ church. The pastor writes a column for the newsletter entitled "From the Study." One month, the last letter of the column was omitted from the stencil.

So, the column, signed by the pastor, carried the following heading:

"From the Stud"

Shared by Gin Shima, secretary
First Christian Church
Loveland, CO

When the pastor of a Pennsylvania church met with the Administrative Board, the then-secretary erred and wrote a headline with transposed letters:

"Pastor John Meets With the Broads"

The same secretary expressed sympathy in another bulletin to the Concord family on the "expected" death of a family member.

Shared by Margaret Gillingham, secretary
Concord United Methodist Church
Beaver Falls, PA

A single letter was mistyped to produce the following blooper for an Oklahoma church several years ago:

"The Inquirer's Group, an informal *F*athering of those interested in discussing the Christian faith, will meet

Sunday." That's one way to increase membership in a local church!

Shared by June White, secretary
Westminster Presbyterian Church
Oklahoma City, OK

The country church was too small to have a church secretary, so the pastor typed her own monthly newsletter.

It usually was typed the last few days of the month, but Easter fell the last Sunday, so she was consumed with Holy Week services and tried to finish the newsletter in a single afternoon.

She intended to write a column describing the Easter season and its meaning. She typed one sentence to describe Jesus' revelation to his disciples before his ascension. But, instead of typing about Jesus revealing himself, she mistyped:

"Our risen Lord *relieved* himself in many marvelous ways before his ascension."

One parishioner asked, tongue-in-cheek, if that represented the "trickle-down effect."

Shared by Rev. Mary L. Ricketts, pastor
Edmeston United Methodist Church
Edmeston, NY

A pastor in the tropics was being dive-bombed by a bat at nose level. Perplexed, he continued his sermon as the bat flew closer and closer to his head. Finally, the bat tired and landed behind the pastor. Although the bat was directly behind her, the organist was a woman of considerable proportions who was certainly not frightened by such a small animal. In fact, she slipped off her sandal and with a single blow, felled the mammal. There was a brief pause in the sermon as the pastor turned to see what happened, took it all in with a gasp, and then continued.

Shared by Rev. Richard Breuninger,
United Methodist pastor
Oneonta, NY

In announcing a reunion of those who had attended the Ultreya meetings, the church secretary wrote: "An Ultreya will be *hell* in First Church."

Shared by Ann Whalen, secretary
First Lutheran Church
Brainerd, MN

Homemakers! Get rid of the guilt over your poor housekeeping. At a California church, not once, not twice, but three times a church newsletter story carried the same error. Here's how it went:

"Whenever you replace a blanket, mattress cover, guilt or even draperies, do not throw away the old ones. We always need material, worn or torn, for fillers. Fillers we use for guilts which we sew throughout the year. Lutheran World Relief will pick up the boxes with guilts and donated clothing in October."

Shared by Tina Strandskov, secretary
First Lutheran Church
Glendale, CA

"Getting rid of the guilts."

The district dean was surprised to read the account a Washington church carried in its newsletter, the *Harp,* after he addressed Spokane Lutherans about plans for the church. It read:

"As our dea*d* Pastor Gerald Hoffman noted . . ."

Shared by Rev. Robert J. Anderson, pastor
Lutheran Church of the Good Shepherd
Veradale, WA

All you need are several children and you learn quickly about this type of reading. The newsletter was listing qualifications of persons needed to perform in a Gospel Troupe. Among them were "singing, acting, dancing, playing an instrument, *interruptive* reading, comedy, acrobatics, sign language and/or spirit-led speaking."

Shared by Heidi Kirchner, secretary
First Baptist Church
Rapid City, SD

In announcing the fact that volunteer nurses who are members of my church took blood pressures after church, I typed one of my many awkward sentences. I tried to explain that the blood pressures are taken on the first Sunday of the month, but my sentence read, "This is a service of Elm Park that is provided by registered nurses who are members on the first Sunday of each month."

My good friend, Nancy Garrison, who caught the bloop, wrote me a note passed through the choir that read, "What are they the other Sundays . . . Nonmembers? Enemies?"

A New Mexico church, intending to have a pantry raid, instead advertised a "Panty Raid."

Shared by Vernell Barrick, secretary
First Presbyterian Church
Carlsbad, NM

"The water bears."

In describing a renewal service in the church newsletter, the secretary of an Illinois church wrote, "Renewal Sunday was a lifting event. Thanks to Nancy Teeter for gracing the font with greens. And to the water *bears*." You might say the typo "bruin"ed the article.

Shared by Lynne Johnson, secretary
Our Saviour's Lutheran Church
Naperville, IL

The word "sing" is easy to change to less desirable words. The First Baptist Church of Stockton, California secretary learned that lesson the hard way. A headline designed to induce choir members carried this intriguing headline:

"ATTENTION, ANYONE WHO LIKES TO SIN"

The pastor was hoping to have enough singers to compete with the Mormon Tabernacle Choir, but most members took it in stride.

Shared by Victoria Smith, secretary
First Baptist Church
Stockton, CA

They may be elderly, but they aren't ready to fold up!
A Minnesota church carried this announcement:
"Wednesday, the *f*olden Age Fellowship will meet."

Shared by Irene Benson, secretary
Zion Lutheran Church
Buffalo, MN

A Church of Christ pastor who asked for anonymity
nearly drowned his first convert. A seventy-year-old
woman came forward and asked to be baptized by im-
mersion. The pastor was not really familiar with that
procedure and asked friends in the ministry for advice.
They suggested he cover the woman's nose and mouth
with a handkerchief, lower her into the water, and repeat
certain scriptures and litanies.

The woman was quite nervous as the pastor covered
her nose with the handkerchief and immersed her.

Unfortunately, he temporarily forgot what he was
supposed to say. The woman squirmed and began kick-
ing her feet. The pastor quickly brought her out of the
water, sputtering. "I nearly drowned the dear woman,"
the pastor admits.

An Adirondack Baptist pastor attempted to tell the
congregation about an incident in which a local man
nearly drowned. "I had to give him artificial insemina-
tion" the pastor told the roaring congregation. It was a
few moments until he realized his error.

Shared by William Nunn, administrator
Upstate Home
Milford, NY

A spacing problem changed a famous quote by Martin
Luther King Jr. that appeared in a New York Unitarian
newsletter. The quote read:

"In justice anywhere is a threat to justice everywhere."

Shared by April Gates, secretary
Unitarian Universalist Society
Oneonta, NY

The church newsletter was supposed to seek the owner of a bowl left after a dinner. Instead, the message read: "Someone left a green bowel" in the kitchen.

Shared by Jeanne R. Leedy, secretary
The Dalles United Methodist Church
The Dalles, OR

Fresh New Alternatives to Fertility

"Baby fat"

(See page 42)

4

A Canadian native had pastored the York, Pennsylvania Lutheran church for about three months when the church secretary was typing the bulletin from a dictaphone. It was Mother's Day and the bulletin cover showed a Picasso drawing of a Madonna nursing her infant.

The sermon theme Rev. Ross selected was "Fresh New Alternatives to Futility." Unfortunately, his Canadian accent blurred the title. Appearing in the bulletin was the following:

"Fresh new Alternatives to Fertility."

The pastor apologized after delivering his sermon for disappointing those who were looking for conception alternatives.

Shared by Donna J. Rawhouser, secretary
St. Matthew Lutheran Church
York, PA

The title of the sermon at the First United Methodist Church was posted on the bulletin board in front of the church. It read, "Which Position Do You Want?" Directly across the street, the movie marquee advertised the current movie. It was "Compromising Positions."

Shared by Betty L. Whittemore, secretary
First United Methodist Church
Oneonta, NY

It was Friday and the church secretary was typing the bulletin. She called to the pastor in an adjoining office, "What's the sermon title?" He replied, "It's the same as the one I gave you yesterday." He intended to tell her he had written the title and put it on her desk the previous day.

But neatly typed after the sermon listing that Sunday appeared this title:

"It's the Same As the One I Gave You Yesterday."

Shared by Pauline Gergel, secretary
First United Presbyterian Church
Oneonta, NY

The title of a sermon in a Virginia church was humorous only because of the circumstances. The co-pastors were often confused with one another except for the fact that one soon sported a beard and the other was clean-shaven. During the summer of 1983, Rev. John Smith grew a beard, and the two became known as the Smith Brothers (after the bearded brothers featured on a cough drop box).

The sermon title the following week was "The Art of Sharing." But, still shocked at the pastor's new beard, the secretary misread the title. Here's what she typed:

"The Art of Shaving."

Shared by Nancy M. Thiel, admin. secretary
Lewinsville Presbyterian Church
McLean, VA

After typing the Sunday bulletin, the secretary of a Pennsylvania church noticed there was no sermon title listed. She checked the rough copy and found it. The title was: "Is Something Missing?"

Shared by Gloria Schrock, secretary
St. Paul's United Methodist Church
Warrington, PA

"And our moths shall shout forth your praise."

Not only sermon titles, but responsive readings can contain humorous bloopers. And they leave the congregation with a quandary: Do they read what's written knowing it is not correct or do they orally make the correction and risk sounding different from those around them?

A call to worship I typed recently should have quoted a biblical verse, but a typo turned it into an insect's cartoon:

"And our *moths* shall shout forth your praise."

During one call to worship, a Presbyterian church secretary mistyped the gifts of life, so the pastor read:

"The promises of God are the *fits* of life."

Shared by Rev. Ross S. McClintock, pastor
Highland Presbyterian Church
Lancaster, PA

The leader's statement during the call to worship on Easter Sunday was transformed drastically by the omission of a single letter. It read:

"This mortal must put on *immorality.*"

Shared by Catharine Milham, Administrative Assistant
Central Christian Church
Wooster, OH

40

A printer's error which was not changed on the proof certainly changed the meaning of a responsive assurance of pardon in a New York City Presbyterian church. The response should have read, "In Jesus Christ we are forgiven." But the congregation read what was printed: "In Jesus Christ we are *forgotten*."

Shared by Deborah Truxal, secretary
The Brick Church
New York City

A Mississippi Church ended its service with this post-script: "The congregation will remain seated while the pastor disrobes."

Shared by Daisy Nethero, secretary
Trinity Lutheran Church
Jackson, MS

A Worcester, Massachusetts church ended its service with the Sharing of the *peach*, instead of the Sharing of the Peace.

Shared by Erika Higgins, secretary
Immanuel Lutheran Church
Worcester, MA

Prayer is certainly good medicine, but a number of churches across the United States reported variations on the same theme. One offered 7 p.m. Vesper Medications.

Shared by Phyllis A. Chaffee, secretary
Waverly United Methodist Church
Waverly, NY

Three churches joined the one above in changing Meditations to Medications. A Minnesota Lutheran church started its service one Sunday with Silent Prayer and Medication. A Lutheran church in Ohio committed the same error, offering a Prayer of Medication.

Shared by Irene Benson, secretary
Zion Lutheran Church
Buffalo, MN

and Judy Ulicney, secretary
Zion Lutheran Church
Youngstown, OH

and Colleen Clemans, secretary
First Presbyterian Church
Coerd'Alene, ID

During a unison prayer of confession at a student service written by seminarians at Wesley Seminary, the congregation read:

"Lord, we have sinned against you and one another. Forgive us for our disobedience and falling *shorts* . . ."

Shared by Rev. David A. Rockwell, pastor
Elm Park United Methodist Church
Oneonta, NY

The pastor took a strong antihistamine just before the service to ease his sinus congestion. Its effects were not felt until the pastor bowed his head and closed his eyes to give the morning prayer.

During the prayer, the pastor fell asleep, and the parishioners fidgeted in their seats as the pause grew longer and longer. He soon awoke, but the congregation doesn't let him forget about the time he bored himself to sleep during one of his prayers.

Shared by Rev. Leon C. Gumaer, pastor
Milford United Methodist Church
Milford, NY

"Baby fat"

I was very pregnant during our annual conference session, and as editor of the daily proceedings, sat at a table at the front of the room where the plenary sessions were held.

One morning, I sported a bright red shirt that read "BABY" in large letters with an arrow pointing downward toward my swelling abdomen. By afternoon, many of the pastors were chuckling as I passed, and the Bishop asked me to stand up during the plenary session and turn around so everyone could see my shirt.

Puzzled, I stood. The bishop then asked one of the pastors, Gary Doupe, to also stand, and I understood the cause of the laughter. He was wearing a bright red T-shirt with a sign that read:

"BABY (fat)" with an arrow pointing to his stomach.

No hope department — A Minnesota Sunday bulletin closed its Mother's Day service with this prayer:

"Help us to see again the high calling of motherhood as a sacred and holy v*a*cation."

Shared by Jan Raymond, member
Concordia Lutheran Church
Duluth, MN

Here's another unison prayer that I changed uninten-
tionally:

"Forgive us for wanting to be Christian without bear-
ing the *superficial* (should have been sacrificial) expres-
sion of the Christian way.

One Christmas, a Baptist church in North Carolina
asked a young man to give his debut organ performance.
The church had been scrubbed and shined for Advent and
the altar area covered with greens and candles.

Unfortunately, the young person didn't realize that
newly-waxed organ benches are slippery. He attempted
to slide onto the bench, and continued sliding . . .

Off the other side of the bench into the greens in the
altar area. Unabashed, he played his piece.

*Shared by Harold R. Price, former Minister of
Music at the First Baptist Church
Rockville, MD*

Special worship services, such as Lenten services, offer
a unique arena for bloopers.

For example, the congregation of a Lutheran church
in Michigan has asked that one blooper become an annual event.

It was Maundy Thursday, and as part of the service,
everything was removed from the altar, which was draped
in black in preparation for the Good Friday service. Here
is the explanation that appeared in the bulletin:

"Following the closing hymn, members of the Altar
Guild will come forward and proceed to strip." The congregation maintained anything but the requested silence
as they left the church that evening.

*Shared by Pat Boyink, secretary
St. Thomas Lutheran Church
Sterling Heights, MI*

During the Lenten season, the pastor was eloquently citing initials for many well-known victories as part of his sermon. He listed VE Day, VJ Day and *VD* Day. He intended the letters to stand for victory over death, but the young people of the church thought he was talking about venereal disease. Many chuckled out loud during the sermon.

Shared by Janet A. Hanberry,
Whose husband, Rev. Donald E. Hanberry blooped
Trinity Lutheran Church
Lilburn, GA

There were six lessons in a study group for Lent. The secretary changed a single letter to type:
"Sex Lenten Series"

Shared by Nancy Jorette, secretary
Trinity United Methodist Church
Philadelphia, PA

Three country pastors were sharing in a joint Maundy Thursday service that drew from six congregations. As one pastor offered the eucharistic prayer, he noticed a fly floating in the wine chalice, which was to be used by the pastors and congregation for dipping their communion bread. He pondered what to do as he served both pastors, who gingerly avoided the fly as they dipped their bread.

He decided to scoop out the fly with his piece of bread. But after doing that, he really didn't know what to do with it. He was wearing a white alb and so didn't want to wipe it quietly on his front. He certainly didn't want to swallow it. As he considered his options, the fly began to wiggle around and took flight.

The pastor whispered under his breath to the two other

pastors "God doth provide" and continued to serve communion.

Shared by Rev. Gary Doupe, pastor
Bainbridge United Methodist Church
Bainbridge, NY

How much postage did it take? During the Sundays in Lent, our church has the tradition of using Lenten symbols during the worship service. One Sunday, the symbol was the nails, which was to be followed by an explanation of why the nail is the Lenten symbol. In my haste in typing the bulletin, here is what I wrote:

"Jesus was *m*ailed to the cross."

The Strike is O'er

"O Holy Nightie."

(See page 51)

5 | The Strike Is O'er

An impending strike at the plant where her husband worked was foremost on the mind of a New York secretary as she typed the bulletin for Easter Sunday. It showed. Instead of typing the title of the hymn as "The Strife is O'er," she typed:

"The Strike is O'er"

Shared by Betty J. Gundlach
Former Church Secretary
St. Stephen Lutheran Church
Syracuse, NY

One stormy winter Sunday, the hymn title selected for a New Hampshire United Methodist Church was "When Morning Gilds the Skies." The omission of a single letter made the title appropriate for the ski country site. It read:

"When Morning Gilds the *Skis*."

Shared by Ginny Schulz, secretary
Wesley United Methodist Church
Concord, NH

The pastor of the Grace Lutheran Church, William Maxon, preached recently about peace. But the choral anthem that followed was anything but peaceful. It was listed as:

"There's A *Bomb* in Gilead."

Shared by Robert L. Anderson, member
Grace Lutheran Church
Loves Park, IL

Morning vespers can change this — A single letter

changed the hymn "See the Morning Sun Arising" in our church to:

"See the Morning *Sin* Arising."

Two weeks in a row, the Zion Lutheran Church blooped when it came to the sermon title and the choral anthem. The first week, the sermon was "Jesus' Touch." It was followed by the choir singing, "He Has No Hands." The next week, the sermon title was "God Is Changing Us." The Junior Choir sang "Jesus Wants Me As I Am."

Shared by Rev. Waldemar Meyer, Jr., pastor
Zion Lutheran Church
Deerfield Beach, FL

During the worship service, a bee buzzed around the congregation, causing some concern. When it landed on a window during the singing of a hymn, pastor Karl Schneider smashed it with the Lutheran Book of Worship. Just as the bee was hit, the congregation sang these words from hymn 145 *Thine is the Glory*:

". . . Death hast lost its sting."

Shared by Laura E. Ulrich, secretary
St. Luke's Lutheran Church
Dublin, PA

The processional hymn in a New York City Church made the congregation stand up and take notice:

"*Immoral*, Invisible, God Only Wise."

Shared by Deborah Truxal, secretary
The Brick Church
New York City

"O Holy Nightie."

An Oregon church listed its solo one Christmas as:
"O Holy Nightie"

Shared by Judy S. Wilson, secretary
Mount Tabor Presbyterian Church
Portland, OR

The hymn was 362, *We Plow the Fields and Scatter*. Here's what appeared:
"We Play the Fields."

Shared by Doris E. Reichley, secretary
St. Andrew's Evangelical Lutheran Church
Perkasie, PA

The first song of the United Methodist hymnal is well-known. But I gave it an interesting twist one Sunday by changing one word:
"O For a Thousand *Lungs* to Sing."

My father phoned with music for Sunday, "Jesu, Joy of Man's Desiring." Obviously unfamiliar with the Latin term for Jesus, the secretary, an eighteen-year-old in her first job, typed:

"Ya Sue, Joy of Man's Desiring."

Shared by Dr. Peter G. Law, pastor
Minneapolis, MN

All were to sing a hymn. However, when the secretary's finger missed the "L" key, the bulletin read: "Ass sing." Everyone did.

Shared by Edwina Kenoyer, secretary
White Salmon United Methodist Church
White Salmon, WA

When announcing a musical singing group for a church concert, the secretary of a Maryland church made a typo that created an appropriate word. She wrote: "Continu*Sing* with our concert series . . ."

Shared by Molly Hoffman, secretary
Bel Air United Methodist Church
Bel Air, MD

In typing the words to the familiar hymn "Onward Christian Soldiers," a Missouri secretary typed the following:
"Forward into battle, See His bnanner go!"

Shared by Helen McLean, secretary
First Presbyterian Church
Independence, MO

The music titles printed in the newspaper ad for the worship service of a Florida church had readers chuckling and wondering about the musician's ability.
A soloist sang "I May Never Pass This Way Again." The choir followed the solo, singing, "What More Could We Ask For?"

Shared by Rev. Drexel V. Mollison, pastor
First Community Congregational UCC Church
Lehigh Acres, FL

During prayer requests one Sunday, the pastor received requests for two individuals facing leg amputation surgery. Following the prayer, the pastor stepped up to announce the special music. She said, "And now, join while we sing that old favorite, 'You'll Never Walk Alone.' "

Shared by Pamela Nelson-Munson, pastor
Valley United Methodist Church
Vaneta, OR

No, it's not really that the choir is terrible. But the church secretary changed the hymn title from "O Happy Day That Fixed My Choice" to "O Happy Day That Fixed My Choir."

Shared by Judy Williams, secretary
Community United Methodist Church
Poughkeepsie, NY

The choir director asked the church secretary to send post cards to members of the choir to remind them of the resumption of choir practice in the fall. But the post cards gave singers a laugh. They read:
"Now is the season to start getting our *vices* in tune."

Shared by Lonny Gulden, member
Peace Lutheran Church
Bloomington, MN

The one-word title of the soloist's piece was "He." But a telephone conversation with the church secretary late in the week confused the issue. The secretary phoned the soloist for her title.

The reply was, "He."

The secretary, confused, said, "Huh?"

The soloist replied again, "He."

The secretary asked, "Just 'He?'"

To which the soloist said, "That's it. Just plain old He."

54

The special music for the bulletin was listed:
"Just Plain Old He."

From the St. Paul's United Methodist Church
Elida, OH

The secretary of an Ohio church apparently didn't think much of the choir's idea to sing one song from the chancel area and another from the balcony. This notice appeared:

"Following the senior choir's anthem, the choir will exit to the *baloney* to sing during the offering."

Shared by Rev. Michael A. Havey, pastor
St. Paul Lutheran Church
Leetonia, OH

A Lutheran church in Pennsylvania offered this blooper:

"The program will feature a *sin*-a-long with Barbara Keim Wandres, Guest Entertainer." The church secretary reported that the entertainer thought the error was hilarious. "This leaves it wide open for me," she said.

Shared by Kathryne M. Hanley, secretary
Emmanuel Lutheran Church
Pottstown, PA

The worship service at a New Jersey church featured an "Organ Pstlude." It generally is soft music, but a whisper?

Shared by Linda Matson, secretary
Zion Lutheran Church
Long Valley, NJ

Members of Holy Trinity Church recently wondered if the piano accompanist was part of a conspiracy to murder the worship music. She was listed in the church

bulletin as:
"Ann Cunningham, accomplice"

Shared by Karen Tomich, member
Holy Trinity Lutheran Church
Beaver, PA

The choir of a Maryland church must enjoy eating. The church secretary referred to the group as the "Snactuary Choir."

Shared by Mary Ann Birch, secretary
Oxon Hill United Methodist Church
Oxon Hill, MD

It does get boring sometimes but . . . A Lutheran church had the "Humn of the Day" listed in the bulletin.

Shared by Pamela S. McKinley, secretary
Lutheran Church of the Good Shepherd
Holmdel, NJ

During her first week as a church secretary, a Texas woman discovered the choir has a sense of humor. She typed:
"Cancel Choir" after the title of the choral anthem. They sang anyway.

Shared by Christy Lamb, secretary
Northwoods Presbyterian Church
Houston, TX

The choir of Washington church joined with five area choirs to present a music festival. When a single letter was dropped, the bulletin message read:
"First Church choir join six (m)assed choir for festival . . ."

Shared by Debbie Allison, secretary
First United Methodist Church
Vancouver, WA

Glory to God in the High Test

"Needle soup"

(See page 64)

6

The late sexton of a Connecticut United Methodist church received a well-deserved reputation for his poor grammar. One Sunday shortly before Christmas, the outside bulletin board read:

"Glory to God in the High Test."

Shared by A. Lillian Thomas, secretary
Prospect United Methodist Church
Bristol, CN

The bulletin board in front of the Highland Baptist Church had two sermon titles posted that had passing motorists chuckling. The message read:

Morning sermon text: *Jesus Walks on Water*.

Evening sermon text: *Searching for Jesus*.

The bulletin board of the Baptist church in Phillips, Wisconsin reads:

First Baptist Church
A. Little Pastor

Shared by H. Conrad Hoyer
Phillips, WI

The front bulletin board of the Central Christian Church in Elmira, New York listed Sunday's sermon as "Cleanliness is Next to Godliness." Passers-by chuckled as they noticed the car wash within 50 feet of the sign.

Shared by Cheryl Allison, member
Central Christian Church
Elmira, NY

The pastor of a Washington church was preaching a

60

series of sermons at both of his services on "The Time of Your Life." But the bulletin board one Sunday was not exactly appealing to potential parishioners. It read: "The Longest Hours — 8:30 a.m. and 11 a.m."

Shared by Dr. William F. Walles, pastor
Mount Cross Lutheran Church
Tacoma, WA

The bulletin board at the Tioga Center, New York United Methodist Church always posted the sermon title. On Sunday, it read:
"The Root of All Evil Is . . .
Rev. Kenneth E. Wood"

Shared by Rev. Kenneth E. Wood
Program Director, Wyoming Conference
United Methodist Church
Binghamton, NY

The United Methodist General Conference in 1980 was held in Indianapolis. To greet the thousands of pastoral and lay delegates to the church, a local hotel chain posted a greeting. It was especially appropriate to the hectic pace of general conference session. It read:
"Welcome Untied Methodists."

Church reports and budgets offer sites for humorous typographical errors. One abbreviation in a Pennsylvania church's budget caused some chuckles. In preparing the 1980 annual report the secretary typed:
"Soc. Sex. taxes . . . $3,000" in lieu of the line for social security taxes that year. When the church council president saw the blooper, he commented, "Well, I don't mind paying $1,000 for social sex, but $3,000 is just too much!"

Shared by Eleanor M. Berger, secretary
St. John's Evangelical Lutheran Church
Kutztown, PA

I'll bet that did cheer them up, though. A blooper I caught before it was printed in a breakdown of our church budget was:

"Flowers and *cars* are sent to the hospitalized."

The outgoing financial secretary of a Virginia church added this note to her final annual report:

". . . my appreciation for the opportunity of serving as financial secretary for the past five years. I have truly received much more than I have given."

Shared by Rev. Mark W. Radecke, pastor
Christ Lutheran Church
Roanoke, VA

The American Baptist Women's report was supposed to end with the lines "We praise the Lord for such a tremendous group of ladies in ABW. It is such a *joy* to work with them."

Instead, here's what appeared:

"It is such a *job* to work with them."

Shared by Heidi J. Kirchner, secretary
First Baptist Church
Rapid City, SD

The conference report of a New York church was broken up when the lay leader read a typo. In listing the names of the year's United Methodist Women's officers, Sue Hahn's name somehow became Sue Haha. The secretary reports that as the conference was in session, the lay leader burst into laughter and remarked that the United Methodist Women must not be taking their activities very seriously.

Shared by Georgia Reeve, secretary
Centerport United Methodist Church
Centerport, NY

62

The secretary was reminding Council members of election procedures. Here is what she said:

"The two people with the highest number of votes will be elected to three-year terms. The person with the next highest number of votes will be *sentenced* to the one-year term."

Shared by Rev. Robert B. Lineberger, pastor
Lutheran Church of Our Saviour
Richmond, VA

It was time for the submission of the New Jersey Lutheran Synod's annual bulletin of reports. The guidelines sent to committees, institutions and divisions carried this underlined beaut:

"Please be careful with spelling and *grammer*."

*Shared by Rodney Felder
President, Upsala College
E. Orange, NJ*

The 134th annual report of an Iowa church left questions as the church moderator's report was read. It said:

"Pastors Frank and Wilmer must have been loyal in their support of the ministries under their *car*."

*Shared by Donna Green, secretary
First Baptist Church
Des Moines, IA*

In a report listing priorities of the coming year, I managed to create a humorous blooper. One of the priorities was to encourage members of the church to use the library. Here is what I typed:

"Priority 5 — Make better use of the librarian."

The church librarian, young and nice looking, luckily did not notice.

Was the Holy Ghost there? At the quarterly business

meeting of Massachusetts Baptist church, the secretary stopped further business when she read that the Massachusetts Baptist Convention was held in the "Newton Theological Cemetery."

Shared by Olive Demarini, secretary
First Baptist Church of Mendon
Mendon, MA

Is your church this friendly? In a budget listing how the worship funds are spent, I typed:
"Congregational life is celebrated in and through worship and *feeler*ship experiences."
A Baptist secretary ended a letter with this closing:
"May the Lord bless your *lice* richly."

Shared by Evelyn Lord, secretary
First Baptist Church
Minneapolis, MN

Barbara Burger, secretary of the Palm Lutheran Church in Palmyra, New York, calls in information for a weekly insert of a local merchandizing paper. One week, a new typesetter with little knowledge of the church year was on duty. Although the secretary spelled all of the words for her, the typesetter still made an error. Instead of typing Church Triumphant, the insert said:
"Those who have entered the *church try outs* will be remembered by name in prayer."
Wonder what qualifications and skills are required?

Shared by Carol Steinhart, secretary
Holy Trinity Lutheran Church
Hershey, PA

Timing is everything — the ***Christian Century*** carried an advertisement for an organist that kept readers thinking. It read:

"UCC Church with well supported music program seeks three-quarter time organist . . ."

The Warren, Pennsylvania, community newspaper was supposed to advertise a preschool. But the ad's headline was changed to promote "St. John's *priest* school," stating that children participating had to be "four years old by September 30."

Shared by Gary W. Tremblay, member
St. John Lutheran Church
Warren, PA

The menu of a bazaar at the St. Paul Lutheran Church as advertised in the Port Clinton, Ohio *News-Herald* didn't whet many appetites. It read:

"Menu for the day includes homemade chicken *needle* soup."

Shared by Martha E. Jonas
Upper Sandusky, OH

"Needle soup"

The marketing director at C.S.S. Publishers was chagrined when he re-read a promotional flyer on a book entitled *Help me God! It's Hard to Cope.* Under a photograph of the book ran a quote from its text that sounded perfectly innocuous, but brought many comments later. It read:

"Don't let worry kill you — let the church help."

The First Baptist Church was featuring the Parable Players, a religious drama group. The local newspaper took the announcement via telephone. Here's how it came out:

"The Terrible Players will be presented at 7:30."

Shared by Dr. Robert H. Thurau
Franklin, PA

The church newsletter of the Bethel and Grace Lutheran Church carried this interesting ad for a church secretary:

"Ability to *typle* is the primary requirement, with accuracy being more important than speed."

Shared by Rev. Heidi Kvanli, co-pastor
Bethel and Grace Lutheran Church
Palisade, MN

There's
a Fly
in My
Communion Cup

"Will he make it to 'I do'?"

(See page 70)

7

Wedding and communion services offer arenas for situations that break the solemnity of the moment.

One classic offered by a New York pastor resulted from the acute shyness of the bridegroom. Crowds of people made him tongue-tied, but as is often the case, their "family-only" wedding soon swelled to a massive affair.

The groom cautiously made his entrance and the pastor noticed that, during his homily, the groom was tugging on his collar and his complexion matched his dove-gray tuxedo. The marriage service suspended as the bridegroom was seated. His jacket and vest were removed, and his collar unbuttoned. The bride, standing alone now, looked concerned.

During this break, the organist played a hymn, but as soon as the groom stood up again, the organist rushed off through a back door to seek smelling salts.

The proceedings continued, but when the groom again became faint, his shirt was unbuttoned and he was fanned by his parents. He just choked out the "I Do," and was struggling with the other vows, when the bride burst into tears.

Rather than prolong the couple's agony, the pastor raised his arms for the benediction, the cue for the organist to begin the recessional. The organist was still out looking for smelling salts. Emphasizing his cue again, the pastor once again looked to the organ and raised his arms. Just then, the organist returned, saw the situation, slid onto the organ bench as though it were home base and pounded into the recessional.

Shared by Rev. Richard Breuninger
United Methodist Pastor
Oneonta, NY

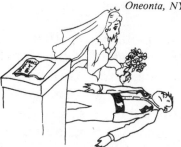

"Will he make it to 'I do'?"

A marriage bulletin for a Connecticut couple's wedding provided some interesting instructions to the congregation:

"Will you also offer a prayer that God's blessings may rest upon this couple who are at this time being *untied* in the Holy estate of Christian marriage."

Shared by Barbara Sandlin, secretary
St. Luke Lutheran Church
Gales Ferry, CT

Rev. Herb Bowen, the pastor of the Cooperstown United Methodist Church in New York said one wedding he conducted by candlelight resulted in humorous tragedy. Surrounded by candles, the cleric raised his arms to give the benediction. "You're on fire," hissed the bride. Rev. Bowen quietly flapped his arms to extinguish the flame and the wedding ended.

It was a newly-ordained pastor's first wedding. The ceremony was scheduled for 1, so Pastor McCall was at the church at 12:30. No one arrived by 1, and the pastor began to wonder if he had written the wrong date. He checked his calendar, and the date was correct. By 2, he figured the wedding was called off. He dialed the bride's home, and, in a concerned voice, asked if they were coming. The bride's mother laughed. "Oh, yeah, I guess we should have called you. We're still finishing the macaroni and potato salads." The couple and family arrived at 4:02 and the wedding ceremony went smoothly. He learned that small towns do not stand on ceremony.

Shared by Rev. William McCall
United Methodist Pastor
Worcester, NY

A wedding at the Vestal United Methodist Church tickled guests. When the father of the bride was asked, "Who gives this woman?" he responded, "My mother and I do."

Shared by Rev. Gary Doupe
United Methodist Pastor
Oneonta, NY

When a pastor became tongue-tied at a wedding, he asked the bride-to-be if she would take her fiance as her wedded *wife*. Disgusted, the bride repeated her vows testily, saying, "I take . . . to be my wedded *husband*."

Shared by Rev. Breuninger

It was one of the first weddings the newly-ordained female pastor had conducted. With the couple kneeling before her, she raised her arms to give the benediction. The bridegroom, not rehearsed in this part of the ceremony, flinched and moved back, thinking she would hit him as she crossed herself. "Imagine, a man being scared of me — not even 120 pounds," she said.

Shared by Rev. Patricia A. Haven, associate pastor
First United Methodist Church
Oneonta, NY

Rev. Gary Doupe was pleased to serve as organist at his mother's marriage ceremony, and as an ordained minister also assisted during the ceremony. He played the prelude and moved to join the other pastor at a makeshift altar area of a bench suspended on blocks. As he did, the weight change caused the bench to begin to go backwards and it fell with an echoing crash. After a long breathless pause, Gary told the congregation sheepishly, "Well, it makes a fellow nervous to marry his mother."

While serving a Lutheran church in Montana, the pastor officiated at a large wedding that the tiny church would not accommodate. A nearby Disciples of Christ church was used. The pastor asked an usher to help move a kneeler into place.

Mistaking the filled baptistry for a shiny floor, the usher fell into the water with a resounding SPLASH! The dripping man was assisted by the pastor to his office, where the pastor gave the usher his pants and donned a floor-length robe to cover his legs. No one was aware of the bottomless pastor.

Shared by Rev. Thomas D. Morgan
Lutheran pastor
Kenner, LA

Couples in the Georgia church were renewing their marriage vows, led by the pastor and his wife, who had been married thirty years and were the Georgia contact clergy couple for Lutheran Marriage Encounter. During a solemn moment, the pastor and wife faced one another and joined hands. The pastor was supposed to renew his promise to be a loving partner. Instead, the pastor, in front of a full 11 a.m. congregation, told his wife, "Jan,

I now *renounce* my promise to be your loving partner." Seeing her shocked look, he quickly corrected the error.

Shared by Janet A. Hanberry
Trinity Lutheran Church
Lilburn, GA

A pastor known for accidental slips of the tongue expressed appreciation for the altar flowers. They were left from the Saturday wedding of a young couple from the congregation, he said. But that wasn't enough. He went on to say, "Yesterday, at this very time, at that very spot, their marriage was consummated."

Shared by Rev. William Lawrence, pastor
Owego United Methodist Church
Owego, NY

Not only weddings, but communion services can provide behind-the-scenes humor. Seminaries may not include courses on dealing with the unexpected, but pastors quickly learn that anything that can happen probably will. Rev. Rees Warring, now pastor of the Elm Park United Methodist Church in Scranton, Pa. shares two examples:

Rees was serving a tiny country church and in the summer. all the windows were kept open, which resulted in a myriad of flies in the sanctuary. One Sunday, Rees lifted the communion tray lids during the prayer. He was appalled to discover dead flies in nearly every communion cup. It was too late to stop the service, so he offered a very *long* prayer, and flicked every fly out of the cups.

Communion continued and not one member of the congregation suspected anything out of the ordinary.

In another church he served, an older gentleman came forward and knelt at the communion rail. As he ate the bread, he sneezed and his dentures flew across the

74

communion rail. Still praying, Rees pulled a handkerchief from his pocket, picked up the dentures, handed them back to the red-faced man, and continued the service.

Now, that's acting coolly.

A Pennsylvania secretary changed the communion elements one Sunday to convince the two pastors that they were serving prisoners. She typed:

"All those who believe with us that God's gracious gift of forgiveness comes to us in and with the elements of bread and *water* are welcome to commune with us at any time."

This was the secretary's first bulletin after she was hired.

Shared by Shirley Hirschel, secretary
St. Paul's Lutheran Church
Catasauqua, PA

In Jamaica, beetles grow much larger than here, and a huge armored beetle was discovered by a pastor on the communion table. Undismayed, he covered the insect with the lid to the communion tray. All went well until the lid began to float toward the edge of the table, and was in danger of falling noisily.

The pastor held the lid down with his elbow and continued serving communion. But there were some members of the congregation chuckling as they came forward to receive the elements.

Shared by Richard Breuninger

Sometimes it's a battle, but . . .

A Lutheran church listed a marriage class as a "martial meeting."

Shared by Robert L. Anderson, member
Grace Lutheran Church
Loves Park, IL

The
Dead
Shall Rise

"He's alive!"

(See page 77)

8

Just as each church secretary has at least one humorous typo to share, so most pastors have amusing anecdotes from their ministry. Here are a few in addition to those already interspersed throughout the book:

"He's alive!"

Leon Gumaer, a United Methodist pastor, was asked to conduct a commital service more than an hour and a half away from his parish. By the time he arrived, a flu had him feeling as though the Chinese Army was having a pogo stick derby on his head and stomach. He suffered through the service, but was looking a little green. The funeral director suggested he stretch out in his hearse to rest a bit. Leon did, and promptly fell asleep. He awoke when the vehicle stopped. Taking a few minutes to fully awaken, he slowly sat up and drew the side curtain to see where he was. He was face to face with a gas station attendant, who was surprised and shocked to see a body in the back of the hearse staring back at him. The gas pump flew into the air, and the attendant ran on shaky legs to the service station, as the funeral director tried to catch up to explain the situation.

Leon also joined a number of other pastors in slipping into a grave. It happened at the funeral of an elderly parishioner with no family. Only a half dozen geriatric friends were at the service, so the pastor helped the funeral director to place the casket. Now, Leon is a man of considerable proportion, and his weight broke the plank across the grave. He struggled to keep his composure and prevent the casket from tilting. Finally, the casket was balanced and Leon scampered out of the hole to conduct the service.

This one was told to pastor Mike Wilson by a theology professor, Horace Allen. The Anglican church revived an Easter vigil celebrated in the early church. An elderly priest was broadcasting the historic event live on national radio from the National Cathedral. The liturgy was very long, and the priest did not have the passage memorized. Word by word, the commentator described what was happening.

"Father _____ is now adding oil to the holy water," he said. Just then, the pinch-nosed glasses the priest wore fell into the solution he was mixing. Unceremoniously, he whispered "Oh, shit."

Without missing a beat, the commentator ad libbed, "Now the cleric is saying that ancient chant — oh shito ergo practo." No one but the commentator, the priest and a few assistants were any wiser.

The pastor had been dieting and managed to lose several pounds. As he raised his arms to pronounce the benediction, his pants fell to the floor. Since he was behind the pulpit, he merely kicked the pants under the pulpit and walked out. His long robe covered his faux pas.

When a district superintendent, whose father was also a pastor, was much younger, he and his brother were holy terrors. As they cut up in front of a member of the church his father served, the layman asked the pastor why his sons were so devilish. Wryly, the older pastor replied, "Because they only have the laymen's kids to play with, of course."

Shared by Rev. Douglas N. Akers,
Oneonta District Superintendent
United Methodist Church
Sidney, NY

Graffiti seen on the school locker of the son of a United Methodist preacher:
"John Doupe's father is a nun."

Shared by Rev. Gary Doupe

Speaking of nun, William Nunn, who directs the Upstate Children's Home in Milford, New York loves to introduce himself this way:
"To my knowledge, I am the only Nunn who's a United Methodist serving a Baptist home."

When a United Methodist pastor first went to a new parsonage, there was little furniture. The previous pastor furnished his own bedroom furniture and took it with him. So, for a time, the pastor and his wife slept on a fold-out couch. After several weeks, the laymen of the church purchased an antique oak bed frame for $12. The box springs were also purchased, but the bed still lacked a mattress. In church that Sunday, the pastor tried to thank the congregation for its efforts, but here is what he said:

"Well, Sue and John went out and bought us a bed, and we have the springs now too. So Mary and I are working on a mattress."

The congregation roared.

Shared by Rev. Richard Breuninger

The pastor was announcing a guest preacher for the following Sunday. Urging parishioners to come, he said it isn't fair for a guest to carefully prepare a sermon for a congregation that "is only half there."

Shared by Glenn E. Bigelow, member
St. John's Lutheran Church
Belleville, PA

A United Methodist pastor was good friends with an Irish Catholic who happened to own a local restaurant-tavern. The friend asked the pastor to perform a commital service for a relative, and the pastor readily agreed. The tavern owner told the pastor to come by the bar for a ride to the commital service. As the pastor walked into the bar, a congregation member saw him and quipped, "Starting a little early today, aren't you?"

Unashamed, the pastor went into the bar, caught a ride to the service and then was invited back to the restaurant for dinner with the family. He entered the bar through a back door, and was witnessed by another parisioner. As he was leaving the dinner, he started out the front door. The local Baptist minister was driving by, and the United Methodist pastor waved a greeting. As he did, he missed the top step and rolled out onto the sidewalk.

"I'm sure they must have thought I really drink a lot," the pastor laughed.

Shared by Leon Gumaer

When the pastor called the home of a member of the Pastor-Parish Relations Committee to give a reminder about an upcoming meeting of the group, her teenaged son answered. The pastor gave the message with the time and date of the meeting. When the committee member arrived home, here was the son's message:

"Pastor *Perish* Relations meeting Monday at 7."

Shared by Rev. Patricia Haven

A Pennsylvania pastor lived in a parsonage with a windowed landing halfway down the stairs. He had recently been chastised by a local funeral director for not answering his phone when a parishioner died and the director could not contact him.

As he showered one morning shortly after that, the pastor heard the phone ringing, and, remembering the funeral director's words, ran out without so much as grabbing a towel to answer the telephone.

As he ran down the stairs, he lost his footing, and fell out the window to the shrubs below.

Who was out walking his dog early in the morning but that same funeral director. "Good morning, pastor," he said, as the pastor, remaining behind the bush mumbled something less than "G" rated and then slipped into the house.

Shared anonymously
Since the pastor is a counselor now